MAX IS MISSING

Peter Porter arrived in Britain fifty years ago and has lived there ever since. Since 1974, he has visited his native Australia often and considers himself part of the present-day poetry worlds of both nations. Since 1968 he has been a freelance literary journalist and reviewer. He has published sixteen books of poems, plus four further volumes with the Australian painter, Arthur Boyd. He has two daughters and, together with his second wife, eight grandchildren.

MAX IS MISSING
PETER PORTER

PICADOR

First published 2001 by Picador
an imprint of Pan Macmillan Ltd
Pan Macmillan, 20 New Wharf Road, London N1 9RR
Basingstoke and Oxford
Associated companies throughout the world
www.panmacmillan.com

ISBN 0 330 48698 5

Typeset by SetSystems Ltd, Saffron Walden, Essex
Printed and bound in Great Britain by
Mackays of Chatham plc, Chatham, Kent

For Evan Jones

Contents

Acknowledgements, xi

Last Words, 3

Deo Gratias Anglia, 4

Streetside Poppies, 5

In Paradisum, 7

Late Lines, 9

Max is Missing, 10

Orlando's Parrot, 12

Come Close My Eyes, 13

The Sydney Spiders, 14

A Butterfly Stampede, 15

Reinventing the Wheel, 17

The Puppy of Heaven, 19

Servants of the Servant of the Muse, 20

The Atheist's Comedy, 22

The Undarken'd Ray, 24

The Last Hours of Cassiodorus, 26

Le Patron Mange Ici, 27

So Unimaginably Different and
  So Long Ago, 28

Antonio Soler's Fingertips, 29

Old Friends, 31

Streamers, 33

The Kipling Donkeys, 34

The Lost Watch, 35

Calumny, 36

Tasso's Oak, 38

A Lido for Lunaticks, 40

The Philosophers' Garden, 43

Clichés as Clouds Above Calstock, 46

Scrawled on Auden's Napkin, 48

Confessional, 50

The Man Who Knew Everybody, 52

The Sweet Slow Inbreak of Angels, 55

The Man With the Blue Catarrh, 56

Magica Sympathia, 58

Sir Oran Haut-Ton on Forest
    Conservation, 60

Favourite Islands, 62

Hermetically Sealed or
    What the Shutter Saw, 65

Duetting With Dorothea, 68

A Pleaching of Spoonerisms, 71

Ex Libris Senator Pococurante, 72

Lichtenbergers, 75

Acknowledgements

Thanks are due to the editors and compilers of the following magazines, periodicals and anthologies in which some of these poems appeared: *The Age, Melbourne; Ambit; Antipodes; The Australian's Review of Books; Critical Survey; Eureka Street; Kunapipi; Last Words* (Salisbury Festival, 1999); *Meanjin; New Writing 9*, edited by A. L. Kennedy and John Fowles; *Newcastle Poetry Prize, 2000; The Poetry Review; Rialto; Return to Kerguelen* (Vagabond Press); *Sight Lines; Tertulias Hispano-Británicas,* 1999; *Times Literary Supplement; Verse.*

MAX IS MISSING

Last Words

In the beginning was the Word,
Not just the word of God but sounds
Where Truth was clarified or blurred.
Then Rhyme and Rhythm did the rounds
And justified their jumps and joins
By glueing up our lips and loins.

Once words had freshness on their breath.
The Poet who saw first that Death
Has only one true rhyme was made
The Leader of the Boys' Brigade.
Dead languages can scan and rhyme
Like birthday cards and *Lilac Time*.

And you can carve words on a slab
Or tow them through the air by plane,
Tattoo them with a painful jab
Or hang them in a window pane.
Unlike our bodies which decay,
Words, first and last, have come to stay.

Deo Gratias Anglia

England where the natives speak in iambic pentameter.
PRESTON MERCHANT

So when the moon is high an ancient spell
Falls on the sons of Milton, Donne and Pope
And Londoners converse in perfect numbers.
Dismantled orthodoxy goes on dreaming,
Its baffled children feeling on their faces
One light and then one heavy drop of rain.

Streetside Poppies

After fifty years of writing poetry
I lust still for what is natural.

My vernacular was always bookish;
somehow I missed the right Americans,

I couldn't meld the High and Low –
even my jokes aspired to footnotes –

but I am open to Wordsworthian signs.
Along the Via Flaminia the whole

of Rome's rebuilding, cobbles
like liquorice blocks in Piazza del Popolo

and flowering by a building site
'a thin red line' of city poppies.

Time to abort my years of affectation:
burn, you petals, confront Bernini,

remember the queue of conquerors
from Alaric to General Clark.

History has clogged the open city
of the heart: it's sixty feet above

its early certainties and I
can visit churches only for the Art.

The rain's been heavy and the scarlet
of the poppies is flambeau'd along

the verge's dark viridian.
Nature, with Roman gravitas,

draws eyes away from angel angles
down to a footsore gallantry of blooms.

In Paradisum

The human body's a barometer
measuring the density of angels
and we who live in flats above the street
give readings of the preternaturally
miraculous. So many times I've listened
in the circling heat of Rome to the same
concise and consonant array of notes
from the piano in the neighbouring flat.
'Ah, Schumann's "Papillons",' I've said,
and next morning with authority,
'He's playing Schumann yet again,'
and on the following day, 'Well, Schumann seems
quite at home in the Trastevere.'
My daughter's neighbour will never get to be
a virtuoso pianist however long
he practises: not up to speed, phrasing
ragged, confusion in his pedalling.
It seems as if this brave *Klavierkenner*
is pioneering Minimalism, his
repetitions and untidy sequences
the Ladder of Perfection's missing rungs.
Suddenly (*plötzlich* in Rilke's angels' way),
The Kingdom of the Equable appears,
and all the rubs of genius cease to count –
the being here, the doing that, the brain

which must abide the body – no, it's Spirit's
paradise, and through his tangled notes
we seem to hear the *chorus angelorum*
and the end of time, with pauper Lazarus
beyond need or call of resurrection.

Late Lines

Miscellanies as far afield as Tottel
Asserting death's the answer to life's quiz
And Philip Larkin with the second bottle
Pouring, saying, 'This is all there is' –

These are the texts to suit the temperament
Of a septuagenarian on holiday –
The sun and stinging-flies both heaven-sent,
The topless beauties spread around the bay.

Watching the écrivisses swim in their tank,
The old man thinks he hears their boiling screams,
No Nobel Beckett, just a witty blank,
Dreaming he cries to wake: awake he dreams.

Max is Missing

The stars are there as mathematics is,
The very there of nothing to be proved.

And so we say that theorems rely
On axioms or proof by the absurd.

The stars outshine the tenses, kings on plinths,
And each enigma of the numerate,

While all along our mathematicians fear
They're stalking-horses of an abstract god,

And posit the suspicion there's no room
For rich historic tit-bits in their space –

The big and little of it, shrunk or spun,
A million needle-points, a 'Mono-Ange'.

Out of the corner of Philosophy's eye
A Mathematician's pinning on a post

Max is missing: ginger tabby cat
With white sabots – reward for his return.

The government of integers will wait
While our researcher searches for his cat,

The stars be patient, God donate his time –
A theorem is for Christmas, but a cat

Is for forever. Come home, Maximus,
The magnets on the fridge are slipping down.

The page is Luddite quite as stars are bright,
A ball-point and a brain out-twinkle them.

Should stars know Max is missing, would they guess
How little he must miss them where he is?

Orlando's Parrot

My grandson's lighter-than-air sad parrot
Loiters out of breath, its head scarce held
Above the carpet, its gaze still heavenwards.
The gods come down to this when their bright thrust
To weightlessness subsides and our attention
Returns once more to our aspiring selves.
Yet, looking at its pained deflation, what
May human apprehension bring to mind
But pity at the subdivision of
Existence into rules and miracles –
The one, subduing godhead to the floor,
The other drifting high defiantly?
Return, O Helium God, defy all leaks,
Float the impossible beyond Nature's reach.

Come Close My Eyes

Our evil days grow shorter and the span
Before the century's end is like my own
Encroachment on a timeless hinterland.
It is the weather of the soul and not
The dread of waterspout and Fohn which drives
Each morning mind to dissonance.
I bring from dreams such journeyings
As pilgrims know must be their destiny
And sole inheritance – the endless tunnel,
The cliff-face clung to by imploring fingers,
The dry facetiousness of a novella
Winched to Apocalypse. Why, when old,
Is nothing left to us but blind incitement
To self-accusation? And why the blackened
Countenances of mockers in the Gallery?
A sort of youthful hope remains – the plot
Is not complete, the play has Acts to come,
The guttersnipe caught fudging playing marbles
May be the true Porphyrogenitus.

The Sydney Spiders

That these seraphically pendentive killing fields
should be ethereal and emblematic
yet need precise dispersal of sunlight
to be visible becomes the wayward insect's plight.
The Tennysonian hero rides on a raft of shields.

It is as if the blue were made of viscera
to digest a further Brahms, a cause
within Creation of beauty at whatever cost.
Dead wings in the sun flash like morning frost.
Jael drives a tent peg through the ear of Sisera.

We sight their silver cities when headlights pass
the giant prickly pear and the Strelitzia
to where car-port and clothes-line sharply loom.
Behold the spiders in their high dissecting room
quiring to the Sons of Morning, *All Flesh is Grass*.

A Butterfly Stampede

Softest of God's creatures ganging up
on a loner, toiling stoic
terraces of olive trees –

                    can they be Furies
these companionable shutters?

Could they brave shades of time, so little
and so desperate? Or quiver through the air
in serious rhapsody?

                In history will souls
recall these flimsiest of comrades?

Swarming butterflies at altitudes
above the wasps, serving in an airy tongue
the primal plebiscite:

                    quick go words which match
the needs of mannequins and mites.

In theory these could be that whelming
catalepse of one foot stamping some
disaster's timbre –

              be calm, O urban mind,
such are just farfalle mustering.

A ghost of city man, he cared today
to save a spider from a shiny bath –
so let him cool himself

with fans of butterflies
and pick a grape for Tantalus.

O Nature! O Conspiring Mind! O Capitalising
Poetry! Rise on the thermals of a swarm
of butterflies.

Hadrian's little soul has multiplied
to blot out death as soon as laughter.

Reinventing the Wheel

The age demands that we invent the wheel.
Why not? It wasn't properly done before.
What seemed a wheel undoubtedly proved useful
And ubiquitous – but just because its rim
Was round and, fitted on an axle, could be made
To carry such incriminating weights
As clockwork, prams and gun-carriages,
While offering spokes for saintly martyrdoms,
We should not credit it as a Gestalt.
Each age has one key aspiration – ours
Is to look away from our contraptions
To find the Platonism of all things.
Or, as Browning must have noticed, when
Chromatic sound is all around us, who can
Collectivise the orthodoxy of
C Major? Does anything exist anterior to
Its root abstraction? Nothing is made
Till everything is sorted. But we are lucky,
The template is reborn in everyone,
Creation starts at each implosive birth,
Anno Domini's precisest calibration.
We are before the Fall and falling ever,
Ante Bellum of the Corporate Wars,
Faustian with tampered DNA.

Hardy cried, 'Ere nescience be re-
affirmed, How Long, How Long?' The answer stares
From creatures' stalking eyes, The Third Way's
Pigeon-holes, Murder's *Make it New* –
Nothingness is lost in history.

The Puppy of Heaven

No one to flee from down the nights and days
Or any of the avenues of fear,
Instead, his ailing body and its ways,
An unpursuit grown duller year by year.

He watched those drunk on self-opprobrium
Devise a ruthless hound of flashing jaws
While he feared nothing more than public odium,
A puppy of reproach with velvet paws.

Some sort of judgment comes to everyone –
Mind overtaken by its metaphor
May watch dismayed as in the evening sun
The Baskerville-shaped shadows cross the floor.

Servants of the Servant of the Muse

Brave Servitors! The ones who wrote the wounding letters,
Who threw cream cakes at the waiters, who afterwards
Took their calipers to the exhumation and measured
Schubert's skull; those whose infra-red intrusions
Buoyed up Turner's Carthage and the Muses' labyrinth;
The ones who know, whose bold explainers have
Their own PRs, and every template at their touch;
The accident curators with their louche anthologies
Born of a blackened christening mug; she who dreams
That you are dead, with no ulterior motive
Since you know she doesn't fancy you; choruses
Of fellow-countrymen whose half-truths framed in
Wholly dreadful prose fill up the lines of history;
Pluralist sciatica sending home evasive messages
From the ageing body's exponential nodes;
Toothache and laughter and the second bottle's tears
Forcing a salty edge on blandness; vegetarians who lead
You past the slaughterhouse and cannot guess your dreams
Are the very cordon bleu of massacre; the modes
Of dreaming too, dull pre-echoes of a dynasty
Of self and silence; passion's briefing – death in the stands
When the Cassino Catechumens play the Subiaco Saints;
The watchers in the street, new liveried in madness,
Looking up to catch you looking down; classicists
Glib as libraries asking why you think the gods

Might care for you; lovers encased in nightmare
Turned to Prep School bullies where the south inclines
To darkness; Science which paints by numbers in the brain
Donating fossil-eloquence; The Masters' catalogue
Without a verb, and then 'Nathaniel Flowerdew, Intruder';
Eros himself, plus sideshow, ballet and the memory
Of women shaving legs; patrolmen of the high surprises
Cruising down the allegories to mark a family face;
Garden days, broadwater nights; the Muse of Matinées;
The curtain raised on breath. Bright Seraphim!

The Atheist's Comedy

Variety's the life of spice, words say
Stumbling from the oracle of dreams
Once more misled by sound's confused decay.
This rocky hinterland has only streams
Of consciousness, a whispering seducer
Leads firelit dancers on his gamepath haunt:
Is this, we ask, *The Raft of The Medusa*,
Our education's boast become a taunt.

And that's the lolloping of Heaven's Hounds,
Their hot breath stinks of childhood's aniseed –
They hunt used condoms in your Prep School Grounds.
Ridiculousness is forced to intercede
On every tragic option; fear alone
Maintains its rugose countenance; we die
In earnest but pallidity of bone
Is all the colour of the empty sky.

But don't complain as poets do too much
That while we're doomed we don't rate very high
Among the villains, and that none we touch
Is cured of anything. For how could I
(I dare say you as well) be self enough
To earn as Quisling or as Tamburlaine
A singularity. There go the rough
We knew at school, as natural as rain.

The play ends happily – that is, it ends.
It's left to tragedy to champion hope
And promissory time to make amends.
Sheet-lightning (punning on the darkened slope)
Reveals a joking face, abandoned now
By its fair-weather friend, ironic doubt;
But still for closure keeping to its vow
To see the Inward outed by the Out.

The Undarken'd Ray

Even those wily moralists who guess
    The leaden casket is the one to choose
Attest that fate commands the boundaries
    Of marvels, tropes and ordinariness,
A rather squally way of documenting
    The past's not just another country but
Home to a species utterly remote.

As much as in Sci-Fi we live our lives
    In capsules pelting to the end of time,
Computers stalked by mutant bugs *en suite*,
    The voyage outward like the one within,
A wrapless darkness, and bold history
    An information screen where love and hope
Flare and switch off, ungravitational.

(Ask what they wore when, in Byzantium,
    Heraclius's men stepped from their ships;
Convene a council where the cheese is forced
    To testify against the worms; demand
Which Frock Coats spoke for Darwin and which wrote
    Him calumnies. You gaze into a panel
Neither comprehensible nor persuadable.)

Outside the wonders of a magic town,
    A prairie tabernacle or a Pale
Of Pico's Greek Debaters, mind addresses
    Its diurnal dismalness or at best
Some sexual chance, a kind examination,
    Or even Sunday when the sun turns on
Its taps and Ego-Lion lies down with Lamb.

Such are the brief pre-echoes of the Great
    And Promised Revelation, the reason why
The questions must be asked. Observe the hoard
    Of artist-understanders filling books
And walls with inklings, are they in the right?
    Was Coleridge foxed by Knowledge's advance
Till what time Death shall pour the undarken'd ray?

The Last Hours of Cassiodorus

God is laying his last slate to the roof,
The ceiling of my death is near complete,
The Vivarium must now live up to its name.

Fish in my stewponds circle silently;
Their free captivity is like the soul,
An endless round, then thrashing in a net.

Our state days pinioned in official letters,
The *Variae* of sound administration,
But Boethian birds still shun my volary.

Home to the South, to sad Scolacium
From Civilisation and a Library,
The sea spray drying on acacia leaves.

After me, what further barbarisms?
My pose is prayer but yet my head is filled
With the terrifying dissonances of God.

I have lived well past my statutory days;
The mapping pen has fallen from my hands,
A hundred years or more of beating wings.

Le Patron Mange Ici

To Peter Steele

Despite what Auden wrote
I like plain cooking, yet this turbulence
of scented oil and melanzane drapes
    could deck a Food God's float.

Such near-armorial grace,
heir to well-sucked marrow bones and flints
for flensing hides of marmosets, attests
    a fast-track artful race.

In some dark when ago
it set ambition up – perhaps with fire,
by accident, or when the great shapes slept –
    to outwit time, and so

Contrive a brain it could
call Mind, and there in parallel discover
a working urge for meat, find it enjoyed
    the taste and smell of blood.

From wheat and bean and grape
we still phrase innocence, but when we gloom
at our rapacity we hail the far
    dream of a gracile ape.

So Unimaginably Different and So Long Ago

We who would probably want to remake
or at least tidy up Tracey Emin's bed
and mostly expect to find our pill-dispensers
in some pharmaceutical cupboard other
than Damien Hirst's, or prefer a child's
kaleidoscope showing a rose-windowed
sunburst to a Gilbert and George blood-test –
we, the uncomfortable in our century,
are equally discomfited by this
display of five-hundred-years-dead craftsmens'
masterpieces blooming in six rooms.

We stare amazedly at a Saint Sebastian
by Pete the Poulterer, are bewitched by
a bust of a Medici by Handy Andy
aka 'Hawkeye goes to Florence',
judge if The Filipino Kid or Street-Cred Larry
carries off the prize among Madonnas
doused in blue and dazzle. What is it here
which harries us? We don't believe in progress
yet how can taste run backwards? We walk home knowing,
whichever of its great ones measures it,
the world must fall a God's length short of God.

Antonio Soler's Fingertips

Starting, starting, starting – I achieve
Only this starting, continuously weave
A tapestry my suitors will not leave.

Keyboard Penelope, I spin through gloom
Of the Escorial such notes, each tune
A fresh-cut flower in an airless room.

Into the minor then – mad kings appear
Beside their tombs: listen and you'll hear
The roads of Spain, the mule and his muleteer,

Whispering Italians with their loud fiatti,
Fresco-painters hoping for contratti,
The immortality of dead Scarlatti.

How seemly is it for an ordained priest
To serve his God, Apocalypse and Beast?
But see, each day the sun is in the East.

The way of music is the art to move
And time moves music in its one-way groove,
An anacrusis with no more to prove.

I play all night and pray by rote at Prime.
Christ on the Cross made blood and water rhyme.
Up Calvary my harpsichord must climb.

I had bright longings as a moutain boy
And knew no other than birds sing for joy.
It was the Bishop's lavishest decoy.

A stork's nest on a golden weather-vane.
I looked – a dream – and saw the Soul of Spain.
Thus Don Domenico: 'So *you* remain.'

The Lord Fitzwilliam's carriage won't go slow –
Bravura, nimble fingertips on show,
The Music God's forensic *quid pro quo*.

Old Friends

Caught by your trade – a spacious memoir
elegant as Turgenev could be yours
to spike your life on – but you'd rather,
given the chance, put the thousand
anecdotal types back in their album
and scorch the world your helpless parents
and your early self served up as fate –
you know that Hell and Heaven must be persons,
and love a promise lost in the palaver.

Old friends! Perhaps you really had the gift
of making friends. But long before you lost,
you doubted them. We're packed too tight
to trust ourselves in this existence,
our chafing neighbourliness,
our indiscriminate appetites,
our unposed innocence – and as they grow
they wave us on to nothingness,
these friends who stand between us and the light.

This poem is for them, not lovers,
relatives or messengers of gods.
Friends are the ones who bear the scars
of work and disappointment. Their
martyrdom reveals us to ourselves
as poignant enemies. In wars
of self we have no allies; we know the light
inside our minds is not our own
but a brightness far off, like the stars.

Streamers

To get away, to make your fortune, to lose your virginity,
you hold one end of a coloured streamer
as R.M.S. *Otranto* snaps the paper symmetry
of country, identity and all your loved ephemera.

And if you remember the ribbon roads with their ribbon
    banners
out from a capital city, flaring on the used car lots,
you swap them for Literature and kinsman Arcite's hots
for Emily, advancing his 'streamer', Mars to Diana.

Then the creeks once known to you as spider defences
on the school's Cross Country Run, become the babble
of a Tuscan stream, *torrente* to Serchio's dry tenses.

Now see where something or other streams in the firmament.
Christ's blood, human destiny, language's gabble?
A straight line is not the shortest distance between two
    points.

The Kipling Donkeys

We posed that day together by the rails
Of *Bateman's*, a family party, you and I,
Our daughters, and ex officio a donkey group,
    The camera standing by.

We couldn't know that you would die
Soon afterwards, and cameras are forbidden to mourn
What hasn't happened: ghosts of the walking wounded
    Lined up with the unborn.

Donkeys can tell our charnel natures
By our smell: the girls leaned down to stroke their ears,
And names, who if they'd lived, would long ago be dead
    Lent us their finished fears.

Wars far off and wars inside the home
Are history: the photo hints at symmetries of life –
Kipling's Arras, the donkeys' pasture, and for our entente
    A last rhyme, man and wife.

The Lost Watch

Lost, and by such an unexpected chance –
    Given by a wife far from here now
    Then carefully kept and twice repaired
    In London and Edinburgh, the shared
    Icon of a half-meant, half-remembered vow.

Dropped by a grandchild whose quick glance
    Up the roller-blading blistered avenue
    Doomed it like the toy soldier in Hans Andersen –
    Perhaps it lies in the cat-controlled grass and when
    Found will keep due death-time for somebody new.

Mine and merely a watch! May it enhance
    The great motives of the heart. Five small graves
    To visit: Bach in his Leipzig maturity,
    My mother's lost children found at last in me,
    Time and time's measurers encircled by the waves.

Calumny

The writer who has turned remorse to habit
keeps coming back to his decreed disaster,
his métier, as God's devised by Heine,
the lure of forgiveness and its *alter*,
self-denunciation; and so foreground
is cleared among the mental junk, designer-
allegory, language lesions, doubtful
analogues of Science; his practice like the
widowed Queen's, to be an *underliner*.

In unsophisticated youth he'd settle
at his desk and feel his fangs obtruding
on his lower lip, his copra'd hair appear
along his back of hands, the poison clicking
in his keys, the untrue and the vicious
chastened by his insight – not a career
but yet a veiled vocation, this unswerving
challenge to the everyday by a no one
out of nowhere, fearful and austere.

It was quite otherwise, the world continued
unreformed and his objective satire
forced him to take himself as subject-matter –
Applausus! It surprised him that another
whom he mourned should be a source of favour.
But words like seeds or bullets merely scatter
emotions to the wind and human feelings
follow tracks so general the public
hears its own heart-rending in the clatter.

Spurious erudition goes on winging
its way into his frozen heart, asserting
he is too respectable to die; a
kingdom peaceable as love is waiting
just for him, extinction countermanded.
He can't believe it, always his desire
is for the species to be fenced with calumny
and she he loved there, doing without justice,
her face lit still by self-deploring fire.

Tasso's Oak

Down from the cloistered calm of San Onofrio
Tasso came to lean against his tree,
All Rome before his gaze and every bridge
And house and market filled with dirt, and palaces
The filthiest things of all. The news was better –
Not many days from now he'd been assured
Great Rome itself would crown him laureate,
His madness turn divine and all the madmen
In the world's insanitary pit
Rejoice that of their number, one was recognised.
But where in final vindication would
Innocence survive, some true thing ringed
By nature as this oak was in its bole?
And where was honesty not reliant on
The shifts of fortune? The oak was young or not
As old as he, and stood for what he'd been
When his intelligence was pure ambition,
When nature had a skin which welcomed pain
As soon as ecstasy. The world was business
And the poet an emphatic businessman –
This was the health of things, but everywhere
His gift reminded him that jewellery shone
Like sickness, that blood dried on the fingernails

Of rulers, belvedered with whisperings
In roses or locked where light would never pass.
The fault was Poetry's, those words which clashed
Like blades but never joined the field, the sound
Of truth but bearing no true weight, the brain
Unable to baptise the conquered heart.
It was the poet's calligram to match
Power with imagination, chart time's
Collision with the tongue, and choose among
The many madnesses, state melancholy.
If the mind's locked up for longer than the body,
Attrition's tedium may bring life down
From sacred heights to watch the valley floor
Where men and women do not bother with
The light forever changing in the clouds.
This was his Rome and this was how the oak
Would buttress him, its newness in his arms.

A Lido for Lunaticks

'And Life is over there'
EMILY DICKINSON

Humanity believes that love is its
One inalienable right. Between a Rosalind
In the forest and a weekend Julie Burchill
Is no great distance. Love is the gloriously
Mechanical operation of the Spirit
Guaranteed by bodies made to fit
As by the motor moaning underneath
The fridge – and ever trumpeted by all
But District Managers as safe economy
For civilised existence. After learning that
Love can behave like the Carthaginian
Army; that it rages Racine-wise
Through sensitive and unintending veins,
That Abelard was made to prove his love
By suffering castration – after this
And Laddish magazines which publish love
As geiger counter to the genitals
Or pecking order on the Terraces –
After every piece of counter-evidence,
Love is still the fond infusive hope
Of ugly, injured, normal, apprehensive
Humans.
    This is the reasonable case
Against irrationality – but like the Monophysites

And Nestorians, our hearts, unreconciled,
Will hold our minds to ransom so we die
On some wild lake of wading birds and not
In bed with watchers and heuristic drugs.
The order of our lives is death and we
Observe it in our hopes of living well,
Our mortgages, delphiniums and holidays.
We are appropriated by the moon,
The mincing goddess who will light our path
From teenage helplessness to self-immersion
In Sound Systems. Love's proper face
Will not be authorised but will concede
In waters calcinous and camphorous
A solipsism of dreams – which scope the heart
Anticipates in its projected Heimatland.

Love is the inward journey of the soul.
Angels dance above it, dervishes
Attend, and any god of any hue
Falls on its sleeve as ash on history.
Behold a Team of Lunaticks, the ones
Intoxicated by reality
Who want some moderating ecstasy
To move them in their sunless bergamasque.

Sex is the one thing which
The body, well equipped for struggle, knows
It shares with disappointment; its real fear
Is elsewhere, in a huge compulsion not
Constrained by brain and nerves.
       If as we trust,
Life is over there, then is this love –
This inconclusiveness which orbits us,
A spacious Swiftian teleology
Of backs being turned, and elsewheres to be at?

The Philosophers' Garden

If on your way to The Tomb where today
they are demonstrating how the stone was rolled away
you cross our small North London Park
and by avoiding the roller-blading children
you take a slightly longer route, you'll find
yourself skirting 'The Philosophers' Garden',
a small crepuscular fenced-off area
announcing itself proudly by so grand
a name. No dogs may enter and no children,
thereby blocking off a half of what
philosophers disdain. Tree cover is intensely green
verging on the black; flowering shrubs have left
to join the noisy world and dampness promises
a Schopenhauerian grave-light through the day.
Unlike the voices hovering here, the place
is modest rather as a Corot sighted in
a provincial gallery, and the smell
of dogshit drifts within its purlieus. 'Dog', says
someone in the Peripateia, 'a glance
back at the spirit world', and as for 'shit'
that's what they call 'detritus' if they have
to speak their native tongue. We settle down
on most uncomfortable benches while
the cursive learning we are forced to hear
drones on, so proud of its great outwardness.

From these dark lines the People's Park seems odd
and hardly plangent, with its bouncing balls,
its ice-cream haloes and injunctions to
the fainter civic courtesies. But here
the rotund ones may read the wind: they note
on Ariel's Web a spidery message – *The Rich
can't die! Dishevelled lie in swathes the souls
of the imponderent,* and *Russell's Tiger
is behind that shelf of bellarmines.*
The colder parts of sun are honoured for
their cleaner light and nothing will earn points
unless its jargon is free-standing. Poets
say they think that song is best *moll-Dur,*
but for philosophy the fastened gates
of any Major are the only truth.
Don't speak here of mutability,
or suggest that you learned evil at your family's
breast, at school or at a job – they'll paint
you in an older garden, one outgrown
by this luxurious seclusion, weaned from
the knowledgeable by Eden's balmy weather.
So now you know – it was worth the trouble
to unlock the stiff and halting gate and find
a hosed-down seat; philosophy is what
made sense at the Expulsion: it was a grid

to hang on when the nerves were sheared away.
It sat along with politics to replan Nature –
witness the leaves like helicopter blades,
the sure eclipse of sun. We feel our clothes
for dampness, start to hear the sounds our seriousness
had banished – surely those are buses straining
up the hill; that seismic shift's from trainers
in their thousands after school. Tiptoe
through the gate, rejoin the unaccountable:
our positive despair will always keep
our prisoned bodies fearful of fences.

Clichés as Clouds Above Calstock

Each epoch has its own conception of
The Philosopher's Stone. Ours is the clapped-out
Journalese of everyday made palpable
In water-vapour. Now, as I try to fit together
This unexclusive quayside, the Muscovy ducks,
The outboard motor coming on board, the children
Running up to pay for ice-creams where the striped
Umbrellas are already flapping, I enjoy
A fine reality left untouched by Manet's brush,
Objective proof that unimprovable Man
Is just a nimbus at eleven o'clock
Both in the sky and on the dial. What should
Existence be but another vapour, one of
The plausible met with in our Life Machine?
Hygroscopic words, I tell myself,
Are issuing from simple actions, susurrus
Involuntary as Resurrection, cast
As ancillaries in dark parts of the Bible.

Clever invention brings no profit when
The words we use have unerasable prints
And will be reborn as they are. We ask them
To drift across the sky to save our minds
From conversation, obbligato social ease,
The soup which Rochefoucauld blew on to cool.
Above the cursive writing of the river
Assemblages of ordinariness assent to pose
As customs of the country sailing through.
Which entry in my disappointment's diary
Will make most sense to me? I've been in Calstock
Several calibrated hours and thought no thought
With proper tangents, no outrider skirting
Daily use. We live in a confusion
Of the Arts and serenity of symbols,
And now the clouds resemble boring speech,
Or languid wounds dressed in silent syntax,
Doubling up as entropy and storm.

Scrawled on Auden's Napkin

All the liberal decencies are stained
By hubris of imagined innocence.
Equality, Socialism, Pacifism,
Vegetarianism – we try so hard
But never can forget our armature
Of blood. Even the Church is compromised
And paints a Heaven for its celebrants
Where sins are washed away and the stern God
Of Judgment romps in playing fields.
Yet Manichees are silly too – despair's
Another wish-fulfilling innocent.
Mankind is always hungry, so eat up
Your dish of Paschal meat, pillage the fridge
For sausages left overnight, sink doubt
In one of Chester's 'savoury messes' –
We eat our way to Paradise, if that's
What an afterlife of unreformed desire
Is called. Our all-inclusive sacraments
And our condign obscenities are tooth-
embrasured; Piety and Sacrilege
Make temples of our stomachs; eating
And shitting are Baptism and Burial;
King Herod is Sous-Chef at 'The Ivy', though
We don't eat 'lovely kiddies' – but we do
Insist that for a species whose most holy

Act is swallowing its God a well-made
Omelette is a Christian deed. We watch
Le Jongleur de Notre Dame perform before
His plastic Virgin. The Mass of the Innumerate
Is our rendering unto Science the things
Which are Science's. My pre-prandial prayer:
Give us this day our daily greed lest we
Forget we're made in Thy Most Famished Image,
Lord of Banqueting. Awaiting us,
A *Concert Champêtre* of wise gluttony,
Two saints, Apicius and Caliban,
Uno barbaro appetito happy to
Defy the runes before a decent dinner.

Confessional

He was heard to mutter,
'But still it moves,'
so we shall have to do a little more.
I told the Cardinal,
'Who gives a shit whether the earth
goes round the sun or the sun around the earth –
my job is just to keep them quiet in the ranks.'
He then intoned a long account
of the Church's damage limitation,
heretics in the North poised to shaft us all et cetera . . .
The Grand Duke's proud of him, next in line I'd say
to his cameleopard and his dwarf.
Once in a while I grow sententious,
I've rehearsed a speech I'll never make –
From Scientist to Priest to God
the only law is observation,
but you can never see enough. That dawn in Eden
they looked about them, and we have gone on looking since.
We deprecate that some half-educated priest
thinks Scripture is an instrument, more fool he.
We can change the words but can't affect the sun,
so we conclude more properly there's no way
of proving anything at all. This is murky stuff:
no wonder serious minds are called to discipline
and theology makes better sense than mysticism.

But there will always be the jokier policemen,
those like me who feel the sun's fire on their faces
and can't be bothered with its proper names.
Please, you never-quiet geniuses,
make water run uphill, devise machines
to sing like nightingales or cut off heads,
pole your gondola to the moon – but keep off grass
it's the Church's job to water. One day I heard
a hardline priest in the Confessional
lose patience with an over-zealous penitent
whose litany of impure thoughts was boring him –
hearken to what he told the self-important sinner
in unimprovable vernacular,
'Give yourself a fucking break!'
shocking her from heaven back to Earth.

The Man Who Knew Everybody

Inside his racquet cover
a note from Misia Sert
and the faintly yellow hankie
used to wipe sweat off at the Finals
in Bordeaux – he's rushing home to change
to meet that Englishman who runs
New Verse and who is bringing him a message
from the uncircumcised Auden.

    The decades change so swiftly
this might be the Via Botteghe Oscure
with Roman urchins thick as partridges
about his legs, and the marvellous boy
encountered yesterday beside a fountain
talking to the pigeons. 'I've called this one
Connolly, he's cornered all the crumbs,
and where the hell is Ostia? I'm supposed
to declaim there by the prick-proud sea.'

    While convoys shuddered through
the Atlantic night, his own war effort
was re-reading the established classics –
could all this death be the proper price to pay
so Stendhal might feel sorry for himself
and Flaubert hone his prose?

    Like him those guys weren't queer.

Hard that – heterosexuality in a century
such as this. It'll come back, said the Big Man
in the Villa. Uranian Love is envy,
a sort of Roman twist to Hellenism,
so very gladiatorial.

    What sadness to have lost
American simplicity and innocence,
the Jamesian profile of an honest soul
amid the European shadows. Here
people will perform textbook obscenities
for a chocolate bar or twenty cigarettes,
and these catarrhal frogs are cousins to the ones
which croaked for Hannibal.

    The old philosopher
is partying tonight – 'Dear Boy,
you find me very busy. I'm rehearsing
for this evening – if I put Peggy "there",
she'll be the Speaker of the House
and call them to her one by one.'

    Whatever happens next
there'll be a name to hail, even as far
as twilight homes in Michigan
with floodlit tennis courts. The Thirties,
Forties, Fifties – how many decades still to come?

The evening has grown visionary,
assignations keep on piling up
and haloed in the Southern light there stands
another gawky prodigy to get to know.

The Sweet Slow Inbreak of Angels

Fra Angelico, Elizabeth must have thought,
Widened his city's hard-edged elbow-room:
Its masculinity needed to be taught
That sweetness turns to power in the womb.

Others were picturing hanged men on the walls,
Their Prophets given soldiers' umbered faces –
The Medici, with six not just a pair of balls,
Liked girls to doff their kit to play the Graces.

Victorian poets conjured angels everywhere
From Water Babies to Absinthe's Lord of Doom.
Palpable angels have faded from our air
Leaving us obliquities by Paul Muldoon.

The Man With the Blue Catarrh

I

Dear God, the world is but a pun,
some scrawling on a freshly painted wall

The politics of where to find the sun;
things that dance, that burn, things pustular.

No good can come of this, no good at all,
the night-time seed has grown too floribund.

No line so short but has begun
to bring to star-charts their awaited star.

The missing rhyme is exiled on some shore,
it dreams the Devil's dream, a righteous war.

War like the attrition of catarrh,
the dailyness of one to one.

II

You'd have your thousand stanzas once, a herm
of understanding – now you've just

An inch of versing, apophthegm
of lovers in mosaic, going up

On eagle's wings, frail Ganymedes of dust.
The soul is stretched until it is a wire

For fear to walk on. Then supply a star
for immanence to follow, fire

On headlands, news from anywhere,
each sore throat a '*bocca del verità.*'

III

What are the tunes of morning, which aubade
will straighten out the tangles of the night?

Sorrows drip, some like a downward smoke
or history unskeining through the light

A mucus of the million shades of grey,
and then the spirit of the lake awoke.

Our heads are stuffed with justice so that they
like Roman Emperors may nod

To bloodfall at the end of day.
Storms given names more quickly end as mud.

The blue of sea has rinsed the planet's blood.
Arise. Arise. The sick man is a god.

Magica Sympathia

Lord Herbert of Cherbury
Lounges in a thicket
Like an unpicked strawberry,
Isaac Oliver, pinxit.

Montgomery Parish Church
Keeps all the little Herberts
As terracotta dolls. Which
One is George the Wordsmith?

Magic fills the landscape –
What, here in Wales?
A flowery English handshake
For Llandrindod Wells?

Windfarm propellers' traction
Turns a Lute Book's pages,
Victorian reticulation
Laps Vyrnwy's emerald edges.

Ask the hawks which hover
Over Dinas Vawr's sheep
Who if not Glendower
Talks rivers up from creeks?

Those plush hermetic demons
Who internationalise
Wye and Lugg and Severn
Are worth a Latin phrase.

The Past is why the Present
Is packed for the Co-op.
It is and yet it isn't
That time must have a stop.

O Sympathetic Magic,
Shy fortresses and weirs!
O Forests Green and Stygic,
The wit of Passing Stairs!

Lord Herbert gave his castle
Up to Cromwell's men,
He held himself a vassal
Only to song and pen.

Sir Oran Haut-Ton on Forest Conservation

How can that fallen creature Man conceive
a working life if all his trees are down?

And our authenticists need wood from which
to make their replicas of Quantz's flutes.

Nature was up all night at the Casino
and found she'd given IOUs on Borneo.

I asked the man from the National Geographic
not to describe me as Humanity's close relative.

The ocean breaks out there on coral reefs,
future detergent for the Stock Exchange.

Wary, always be wary! A sleep too soon
and dragonflies have turned to helicopters.

I dreamt that they survived – our inventive
long-forgotten, hairy fabulists.

Peacock put me in an embroidered waistcoat.
This documentary-maker films me shitting.

'They' have their *Eroicas* and *Rings* to chasten them –
our *Symphony of a Thousand* is Krakatoa.

'Thinking of home?' they ask, but I'm at home
wherever stars evade the canopy.

My uncles from the Holocene are here
interred in stones enchauféd by the sun.

Nature votes *Green*. The world may still be saved.
The ballot-box shall rattle with my bones.

Favourite Islands

They are release from reason's deep persistence
Or rather from the rote of mass and state,
Yet they will be pre-eminently
Rational in dealings with their visitors.
Here, the more careful holidaymakers say,
'A meal for ten is significantly cheaper
Than at home, though the electricity goes off
At vital moments and it's so unpleasant
To watch the local children tease an octopus.
We bring with us a grammar of concern,
Holding that scorpions should be left to climb
Behind the bedstead, rat-traps not be set
And going topless make us seem more French.'

In the bay a steepled catamaran
Is what a Hedge-Fund Manager declares
Will fit his doctor's rule that he relax.
Infinite clarity seems to stretch
Beyond the ragged mountains – blue so rich
It makes its point that here pollution
Is transparent – builders work in heat
To have new villas ready for next Summer,
Northern agencies forever on the phone –
A *vendre*, *à louer*, everything on offer
Even nightmare, earache, family tears.
The portly ferry hardly gets beyond
The window every time you look, and down

The beach-path trot the pouting seventeen-
year-olds whose any natural smile must freeze
To keep their disdain cool. But this is not
The Purgatory foisted by the Old
On their inheritors – instead we might
Assume that islands are the parts we've stripped
From our too-self-contained economies,
Not prisons or Utopias or magic strands
For fables of a shipwrecked Christ, nor yet
A scientist's concordance of Gestalt
But inmost territories of Self, relieved
Of any need of vindication, world
Made world by all the whereabouts of change.

Hermetically Sealed or What the Shutter Saw

(A photograph of 1911)

The stifling air of Brisbane, cleansed by time,
Shows the family *Main* Easter-Islanded in sepia,
Slow shutters making them North British as indeed
They were, though stiffly suited as befits Colonials
Steeled for success. Through this the mercantile's
Made magical; it puts a fearful competence
In frame – Behold a portrait truly *feierlich*
And God-like, humanity a Middle Class *ex voto*.

Pater Familias, mustachio'd, dewlapped, forty-four
But seeming sixty, the God Mark Main turns everything
He looks at into Glasgow – surrounded by his family,
His liver undercutting his immortal soul,
He practises Theocracy. He is informing us
That through the doors which whisky opens, soon or late,
Comes Death the Factor, a well-born trader and therefore
Your family must be properly dressed to welcome him.

His stern and English wife, Mae Simms, uncloned
In whitest lace, a Beatrice of new-built Randwick,
Overlooks the paddock of her hopes. She has the discipline
Of Start Again, a cure for each indisposition:
Fate washes us to peccant shores, but we must keep
The absolute commandments – sons and daughters are
what's left of angels in a fallen universe.
The sun shines through us yet we are the North.

– 65 –

Enthroned in pole position on the left,
Their eldest child, their daughter Marion, sets her face
Into a tuneless cameo: dark-skinned and Pictish,
She gives posterity and photographer no hint
She is an anarch of dejection, a humorist
Of hopelessness. Her bust is tightly fronted, balcony
Of soft dictatorship. She is to be my Mother and will stay
Younger than I forever, her hand enclosing mine.

Behind the seated seniors, two sons, Eric and Neville,
Endorse expectancy and youth, the ichor of their promise
Destined never to dry. Waistcoats, watches fobbing off
The larrikin enticement of their sex, they're blessed
With god-like blindness – they will never see their graves
In France. Perhaps none in the group would know them
On death's wharf. 'Magnificently unprepared', a poet said,
But seldom life's long littleness like this.

Dolly and Winnie, indomitable and plastic sisters –
Dolly a headscarfed *Carmen* extra, Winnie the beauty
With a gaze as basilisk as Passover.
Harder than teenage light, their understanding
Of our fallen natures keeps them well abreast of
War, Depression, Real Estate, Survival –
We have to die, they say, but seaside houses
And golf courses shall be our proper recompense.

Little Roy, who will disgrace them all and as
My Uncle Mick will be a Tattersalls Club bookie
After meningitis makes his Proteus, is just in front
Of Edna, baby of the family, a sweet, buck-toothed
Forensic angel – strange that the chief executive
Of God in this our Family Tenebrae should be
The youngest. From birth she'll know how best
To fend off pain with laughter, work and kindliness.

With seven children who will produce only six
Grandchildren, the parental psychopomps beckon to
Their descendent, a paltry straggler of the age
They were so proud to own. Time's not an integer
Of true forgiveness, but perhaps they wish
The world were spiked with magic, and that their
Materialistic gods might hatch on blankness to become
The fattest schoolboy silkworms of their hopes.

Duetting With Dorothea

With strange compelling instinct
We seek the heavy truth
Of new sophistication,
The plenary uncouth,
So now each maker tempted
To raise invention's stakes
Will climb a self-set ladder
To rob a nest of fakes.

We cannot trust the simpler
Magnitudes of love,
We think that skill and falsehood
Are ever hand-in-glove.
A stanza by Mackellar
Goes by with standard whoosh,
Its privilege and parkland
No rival of the bush.

A seedling grown patrician,
She wanted us to hear
That mise-en-scène Australia
Must always be more dear
To us than coasts of Europe
Because it's what we see
As Anglo-Celtic transplants
In Angel-Infancy.

And Patrick, sailing homewards,
Observed her on the deck,
Light-stepping, pissed and wayward,
In lace up to the neck;
He judged her postcard Southland
Could offer no new starts,
Migration prove no changer
Of fixed empiric hearts.

Shakespeare's Captain Macmorris
Asked in his Irish way
'What ish my nation?' Poems
Have no flag to obey.
It's natural our writers
Eyeing up the grants
Are Hi-Tech patriotic –
Australia Fair, Advance!

But Dorothea's Country
Did not seem mine when I
First looked out of the window
With costive childhood eye.
Instead I saw a landscape
Lit up by inner doubt
And scarred by self-attrition,
Not Barcoo Rot or drought.

I need a further stanza
To amplify my sense
That latitude and seasons
Make little difference.
The human creature burgeons
In social permafrost,
Its feral hope adjacent
Some reasoned holocaust.

Dorothea Mackellar's poem 'My Country', written when she was nineteen, before the First World War, has been memorized by generations of Australian schoolchildren. It considers Australia's British inheritance, 'A love of field and coppice,' but goes on to declare 'The wide brown land for me'. Perhaps unconsciously, Dorothea uses the same metre as Lord Macauley in his *Lays of Ancient Rome*. Patrick White, returning permanently to Australia in 1948, encountered Dorothea, drunk and aimless, but still dauntlessly patrician, patrolling the decks of the ship.

A Pleaching of Spoonerisms

We hail and praise you from our childhoods on,
our loving genitors, dear *Mad and Dumb*.

The weary mariners were tossed between
what seemed *The Devil and the Bleep-Due Sea*.

Knowing his Party's ratings had gone down
The Minister addressed the *Near and How*.

There is no question of a *Fosse of Lace*,
our Embassy personifies good taste.

Day Twenty in the Laboratory's diary:
the smoking dogs are looking *wired and teary*.

The Damaged Quarto has an interlude
for kings and queens, *The Shaming of the True*.

Last Words, Waste Lords, no Spoonerism,
just pararhyme's acute astigmatism.

Who's this insisting on *A Clutch of Tarse*?
My Lord Rochester's been drunk these five years past.

The Networks say the public's tired of screwing,
let's have more prime time *Killing and Booing*.

Dame Luck, Lewd Neighbour, Warring Banker –
our words, like us, are full of useless anger.

Ex Libris Senator Pococurante

Carchamish, this tedious performance
our forefathers valued as the first account
of the creation of the world; it seems
no more than a boring battle between
the snakes and the dogs, with comic referees
called gods obsessed by their own dignity.

The Troiliad, just as silly and twice as long,
with lists of heroes, ships and towns,
interfering gods on shortest fuses
and magic implements and animals,
its love-life platitudinous
and its epithets attached like luggage labels.

The Hunnish Wars, a propaganda feast
prepared by an ambitious consul
for home advantage, as full of lies
as tedium. The style is gelid,
the facts fictitious – it deserves its fate
to end up teaching grammar to dull boys.

Summa Cattolica, a sort of Natural History
of Credulity. Should you want to know
the stories of the saints you still might baulk
at being shown their laundry lists and tax returns.
This huge concordance mixes pedantry
with gloating martyrdom and police reports.

The Satanic Comedy, a strange attempt
to draw a picture of the world based on
the machinations of a city council
together with a paedophile's infatuation
with a merchant's teenage daughter.
In three books, Heaven, Hell and Nowhere.

Eden's End. Expelled from Heaven in a war
with guns and bombs, The Devil tempts
God's franchise-takers with his fruits and hisses.
Our classicist author makes Adam a market
gardener while Eve assembles Lifestyle hints
on Post-Coital Guilt and PMT.

The Interlude. In this almost unending
meditation on the life and times of one
banal existence, the author dares presume
we are as self-obsessed as he is.
Its marginal attractions are no better:
country hovels, childhood and wet walks.

Donovan's Demise, the lexicon of Modernism,
its every sentence stitched into the text
like Cash's name-tapes, this epyllion
of solipsism demands that we devote
a lifetime to its study. Properly examined
it becomes the scribblings on a ouija-board.

Lichtenbergers

*(*Lichtenberger. *Abstract noun derived from (1) Georg Christoph*
Lichtenberg, German Philologist and Philosopher, 1742–99, author
of aphorisms; (2) hamburger, *savoury minced beef in a bread roll.*
Therefore: An aphorism in a bun.*)*

Chaos is the ideal of every pattern.
When he moved out of the mirror it disappeared.
'It is I, Hamlet the Dane, an Englishman.'
Lazarus wished he could remember being born.
A landlord's monarchy and an estate agent's republic
'E pur se muove, since all the instruments agree.'
He asked to be paid in metaphor.
As his health got worse he began to see the joke.
The Pentecost, still awaiting translation
George Washington dreamed he was Benedict Arnold, but
    Benedict Arnold had long stopped dreaming.
'O, Mother,' I cried. 'No,' she answered, 'I'm a young
    woman hoping to make a good marriage.'
A billion galaxies but not one extra tense
To lack the talent of one's convictions
A heap of words on her side of the bed
Your other wig, Herr L., 'der Afro'.
I felt unworthy of his good advice.
Who's this beneath the table undoing our flies?
Message on the screen – Total Tango!
He picks his nose. He cannot be President.
Don't complain your art isn't popular – you may be claiming

the very qualities which lead to popularity.

Each love affair starts in fear;

Some go on to satisfaction;

Few to affection.

Man the Artist, God the Scholar

Depression is Death's Immune System.

He told me his poems were living in America.

'But, officer, I'm a philosopher!'

In a Rationalist Heaven there would be no need to create the world.

'Do you believe in God?'

'Would you rephrase that question, please?'

Saul has slain his thousands and David his census-takers.

God, who put the spin on Creation

Poor Fellow, he's vomited the Dictionary.

Another ruffian on the stair –

C'est Vénus toute entière.

The Unconscious finds Consciousness irrelevant.

You may list the dead in any order.